THE SPIRITUAL COUPLETS
OF
MAULANA JALALU-'D-DIN
MUHAMMAD RUMI

Abridged and Translated

By

E.H. Whinfield

Masnavi
Book 6

[ZHINGOORA BOOKS]

THE SPIRITUAL COUPLETS
OF
MAULANA JALALU-'D-DIN MUHAMMAD RUMI

Book VI.

PROLOGUE.

O LIFE of the heart, Husamu-'d-Din,
My zeal burnt within me to write this sixth part!
The Masnavi became a standard through thy influence,
Thy sword (Husam) has made it an exemplar to the world
O spiritual one, I now offer it to thee,
This sixth part of the entire Masnavi.
Enlighten the world's six sides with its six parts,
That it may illuminate him who is not illuminated!
Love has naught to do with five senses or six sides,
Its only aim is to be attracted to the Beloved!
But haply leave may be given me hereafter
To tell those mysteries so far as they can be told,
In a discourse more closely approximating to the facts
Than these faint indications of those abstruse matters.
Mysteries are not communicable, save to those who know;
Mystery in the ear of infidels is no mystery.
Nevertheless, this is a call to you from God;
It matters not to Him whether ye accept or reject it.
Noah repeated His call for nine hundred years,
But his people only increased in rebellion.
Never did he draw back from admonishing them,
Never did he retire into the cave of silence.
He said, "At the barking and howling of the dogs
No caravan ever turned back in its road.
Nor does the full moon on a bright night cease shining
Because of the howling of dogs on earth.
The moon sheds her light, and the dogs howl;
Every one acts according to his nature.
To each one his office is allotted by the divine decree,
And he acts agreeably to his nature."
Art thou thirsting for the Ocean of spirituality?
Disport thyself on this island of the Masnavi!

Disport thyself so long as thou seest every moment
Spiritual verities revealed in this Masnavi.
When the wind blows the grass off the water,
The water then shows forth its own purity.
Behold the bright and fresh sprays of coral,
And the princely fruits growing in the water of life!
So, when the Masnavi is purged of letters and words,
It drops all these, and appears as the sea of Unity.
Then speaker and hearer and spoken words
All three give up the ghost in that consummation.
Bread-giver and bread-eater and bread itself
Are purified of their forms and turn to dust.
But their essences in each of these three grades
Are distinguished, as in those states, so eternally. 1
Their form turns to dust, but their essence not;
If one says it does, tell him it does not.
In the world of spirits all three await judgment,
Sometimes wearing their earthly forms, sometimes not.
The worth of a man depends on the objects of his aspiration.
One day a student asked a preacher,
Saying, "O most orthodox ornament of the pulpit,
I have a question to ask, O lord of learning;
Tell me the answer to it in this congregation.
A bird sat on the top of a wall;
Which was best, its head or its tail?"
He replied, "If its face was towards the town,
And its tail to the villages, then its face was best.
But if its tail was towards the town, and its face
Towards the villages, then prefer its tail to its face."
A bird flies with its wings towards its nest,
The wings of a man are his aspiration and aim.
If a lover be befouled with good and evil,
Yet regard not these; regard rather his aspiration.
Though a falcon be all white and unmatched in form,
If he hunts mice he is contemptible and worthless.
And if an owl fixes his affection on the king,

He is a falcon in reality; regard not his outward form.
Adam's clay was kneaded in the limits of a trough,
Yet was he exalted above heaven and stars.
"We have honored Adam" 2 was not addressed to the sky,
But to Adam himself full of defects as he was.
Did one ever propose to earth or heaven to receive
Beauty, reason, speech and aspiration? 3
Would you ever offer to the heavens
Beauty of face and acuteness of thought?
O son, did you ever present your silver body
As an offering to the damsels pictured on bath walls?
Nay, you pass by those pictures though fair as Huris,
And offer yourself sooner to half-blind old women.
What is there in the old women which the pictures lack,
Which draws you from the pictures to the old women?
Say not, for I will say it in plain words,
'Tis reason, sense, perception, thought, and life.
In the old woman life is infused,
While the pictures of the bath have no life.
If the pictures of the bath should stir with life (soul),
They would uproot your love to all the old women.
What is soul? 'Tis acquainted with good and evil,
Rejoicing at pleasant things, grieving at His.
Since, then, the principle of soul is knowledge,
He who knows most is most full of soul.
Knowledge is the effect flowing from soul;
He who has most of it is most godlike.
Seeing then, beloved, that knowledge is the mark of soul,
He who knows most has the strongest soul.
The world of souls is itself entirely knowledge,
And he who is void of knowledge is void of soul.
When knowledge is lacking in a man s nature,
His soul is like a stone on the plain.
Primal Soul is the theatre of God's court,
Soul of souls the exhibition of God Himself.
All the angels were pure reason and soul,

Yet when the new soul of Adam came, they were as its body.
When in joy they crowded round that new soul, 4
They bowed before it as body does before soul.
Fear of men's censure the greatest obstacle to acceptance of the
true faith.
O Husamu-'d-Din, I might tell some of thy many virtues,
Were it not for the fear of the evil eyes.
From evil eyes and malice-empoisoned breaths
Already have I suffered fatal wounds.
Therefore I cannot relate thy ecstatic states,
Save by hints of the ecstatic states of others.
This manoeuvre is one of the devices of the heart,
Whereby the heart's feet wend their way to the truth.
Many hearts and souls would become lovers of God
Did not evil eyes or evil ears hold them back.
Of these Abu Talib, the Prophet's uncle, was one;
The malice of the Arabs scared him from the faith.
He said, "What will the Arabs say of me?
That my own nephew has perverted me from my religion!"
Muhammad said, "O uncle, confess the faith to me,
That I may strive with God for thee!"
He said, "Nay; it will be published by them that hear;
'A secret known to more than two is known to every one.' 5
As I live in the midst of these Arabs,
It will cause me to lose caste with them.
Yet, had the mighty grace of God led the way,
How could this fear have vied with God's attraction?
O Granter of aid, lend us aid
In this dilemma of the feeble will.
Prayers for right guidance in the use of free will, which gift was
refused by heavens and earth, but accepted by man to his own. 6
This flux and reflux of resolves came to me from Thee,
Else these tides of will had rested still, O God!
By the same fiat whereby Thou madest me thus irresolute,
Of Thy mercy deliver me from this irresolution!
Thou triest me; O give me aid!

For men are as women through this trial.
How long, O Lord, is this trial to last?
Give me one ruling principle, not ten principles!
The whole world flees away from its own will and being
Towards self-abandonment and intoxication.
In order to escape a while from self-consciousness,
Men incur the reproach of wine and strong drink;
For all know well this existence is a snare,
This thought and memory and will only a hell.
Therefore they flee from self to being beside themselves,
Call it intoxication or call it preoccupation, O guided one.
Ere it is annihilated, no single soul
Finds admittance to the divine hall of audience.
What is "ascension" to heaven? Annihilation of self;
Self-abandonment is the creed and religion of lovers.
*NOTES:
1. Koran xxxvi. 32: "But all gathered together shall be set before us."
2. Koran xvii. 72.
3. "We proposed to the heavens and to the earth to receive the deposit, but they refused the burden. Man undertook to bear it, but bath proved unjust and senseless" (Koran xxxiii. 72).
4. "We said unto the angels, 'Prostrate yourselves before Adam,' and they prostrated themselves, except Iblis" (Koran vi. 10).
5. Freytag, Arabum Proverbia, iii. 222.
6. Koran xxxiii. 72, quoted above. "Deposit" is here interpreted of the will, the ability to go right or wrong.

STORY I.

The Hindu Slave who loved his Master's Daughter.
A certain man had a Hindu slave, whom he had brought up along with his children, one of whom was a daughter. When the time came for giving the girl in marriage many suitors presented themselves, and offered large marriage portions to gain her alliance. At last her father selected one who was by no means the richest or noblest of the number, but pious and well-mannered. The women of the family would have preferred one of the richer youths, but the father insisted on having his own way, and the marriage was settled according to his wishes. As soon as the Hindu slave heard of this he fell sick, and the mistress of the family discovered that he was in love with her daughter, and aspired to the honor of marrying her. She was much discomposed at this unfortunate accident, and consulted her husband as to what was best to be done. He said, "Keep the affair quiet, and I will cure the slave of his presumption, in such a way that, according to the proverb, 'The Shaikh shall not be burnt, yet the meat shall be well roasted.'" He directed his wife to flatter the slave with the hope that his wish would be granted, and the girl given to him in marriage. He then celebrated a mock marriage between the slave and the girl, but at night substituted for the girl a boy dressed in female attire, with the result that the bridegroom passed the night in quarrelling with his supposed bride. Next morning he had an interview with the girl and her mother, and said he would have no more to do with her, as, though her appearance was very seductive at a distance, closer acquaintance with her had altogether destroyed the charm. Just so the pleasures of the world seem sweet till they are tried, and then they are found to be very bitter and repulsive. The Prophet has declared that "Patience is the key of joy;" 1 in other words, that he who controls and restrains himself from grasping at worldly pleasures will find true happiness; but this precept makes no lasting impression on the bulk of mankind. When

bitter experience overtakes them, as the pain of burning afflicts children, or moths sporting with fire, or the pain of amputation a thief, they curse the delusive temptations which brought this pain upon them; but no sooner is the pain abated than they run after the same pleasures as eagerly as ever. This is divinely ordained, that "God may bring to naught the craft of the infidels." 2 Their hearts have, as it were, been kindled on the tinder-box of bitter experience, but God has put out the sparks of good resolution, and caused them to forget their experience and vows of abstinence according to the text, "Often as they kindle a beacon-fire for war doth God quench it." 3 This is illustrated by an anecdote of a man who heard a footstep in his house at night, and at once struck a light; but the thief put it out without being observed, and the man remained under the impression that it had gone out of itself. This leads the poet again to dwell on his favorite theme of the sole agency of Allah.

Then, to supply the necessary corrective of this doctrine, another anecdote is told concerning Mahmud and Ayaz. The courtiers grumbled because Ayaz received the stipend of thirty courtiers, and Mahmud by a practical test convinced them that the talents of Ayaz equalled those of thirty men. The courtiers replied that this was due to God's grace, not to any merit on the part of Ayaz; and the king confuted them by pointing out that man's responsibility and merit, or demerit, for his actions are recognized in the Koran. Iblis was condemned for saying to God, "Thou hast caused me to err," 4 and Adam was commended or saying, "We have blackened ourselves." 5 And elsewhere it is said, "Whosoever shall have wrought an atom's weight of good shall behold it; and whoso shall have wrought an atom's weight of evil shall behold it." 6

*NOTES:

1. Freytag, Arabum Proverbia, iii. 270.
2. Koran viii. 18.
3. Koran v. 69.
4. Koran vii. 15 and 22.
5. Koran vii. 15 and 22.
6. Koran xcix. 7.

STORY II.

The Fowler and the Bird.
A fowler went out to catch birds, and disguised himself by wrapping his head up in leaves and grass, so as to avoid frightening the birds away from his snare. A bird of some sagacity came near him, and suspected something wrong, but foolishly lingered near, and began to question him as to his business. The fowler said he was a hermit who had retired from the world and dressed himself in weeds for the health of his soul. The bird said he was surprised to see a Mosalman doing this in contravention of the Prophet's precept, "There is no monkery in Islam," and his repeated declarations that Islam involves association with the faithful and avoidance of a solitary life. The fowler replied that a solitary life was allowed in heathen countries for the soul's health. 1 The bird then asked what the grains of wheat were that were strewed on the trap. The fowler replied that they were the property of an orphan, which had been deposited with him in consequence of his known probity. The bird then asked permission to eat some, as he was very hungry, and the fowler, with much pretended reluctance, allowed him to do so. The moment he touched the grain the trap closed upon him, and he found himself a prisoner. He then abused the fowler for his trickery, but the fowler said he had only himself to blame for his greediness in eating the food which belonged to an orphan. The moral is, that it is not destiny which leads people into afflictions, but their own errors and vices.
The bird's cries to God for aid.
When he had eaten the grain he was caught in the trap,
And began to recite the chapters "Yasin" and "An'am."
Then he began to wail and cry loudly,
So that the very fowler and his trap shook with grief.
He said, "My back is broken by the conflict of my thoughts;

O Beloved One, come and stroke my head in mercy!
The palm of Thy hand on my head gives me rest,
Thy hand is a sign of Thy bounteous providence.
Remove not Thy shadow from my head,
I am afflicted, afflicted, afflicted!
Sleep has deserted my eyes
Through my longing for Thee, O Envy of cypresses!
Though I be unworthy of Thy favor, how were it
If thou shouldst regard the grieves of unworthy me?
What claim of right can a non-existent thing make
To have the doors of Thy bounty opened to it?
Yet Thy bounty had regard to my senseless dust
And endued it with the ten jewels of the senses
Five external senses and five internal senses,
Whereby inanimate seed became a living man.
O Light on high! what is repentance without Thy grace
But a mere mockery of the beard of repentance;
Thou rootest up the hairs of such repentance,
Repentance is the shadow, Thou the shining Moon.
Alas! Thou hast ruined my house and home;
How can I cease wailing while Thou oppressest me?
How can I flee away when there is no living away?
Without Thy sustaining lordship there is no slave.
O take my life, Thou that art the source of life!
For apart from Thee I am wearied of my life.
I am a lover well versed in lovers' madness,
I am weary of learning and sense.
Since my bashfulness is destroyed, I will publish secrets;
How long must I bear this trepidation and anxiety?
Formerly I was covered by modesty as by a veil,
Now I will leap from it under Thy coverlet!
O comrades, our Beloved has closed up all paths;
We are as lame deer, and He as a raging lion.
Say what remedy is there but resignation 2
When one is fallen into the hands of the raging lion?"
The poet then passes on to the subject of the need for constant

watchfulness, in order to avoid the snares of the world, and not to miss the divine blessing whenever it may appear. There is a tradition, "When half the night has passed Allah will descend to earth, and cry, 'Ho, ye that ask, it shall be answered to you; and ye that crave pardon, it shall be pardoned to you; and ye that petition, your petitions shall be granted.'" But all who sleep the sleep of negligence will miss the promised blessing. This is illustrated by the story of a lover who obtained an assignation with his mistress, but when she came, was found asleep, and was accordingly rejected.

*NOTES:

1. See Miskkat ul Masabih, ii. 541.

2. "To God I commit my case" (Koran xl. 47).

STORY III.

The Drunken Turkish Amir and the Minstrel.
Then follow exhortations to undergo "the pains of negation," as they are called in the Gulshan i Raz, i.e., even as the great saint and poet Faridu-'d-Din 'Attar cast away his drugs, to cast one's own will, knowledge, power, and "self" into the unique river of "annihilation," 1 and from that state to rise to the higher state of eternal existence in God. The end and object of all negation is to attain to subsequent affirmation, as the negation in the creed, "There is no God," finds its complement and purpose in the affirmation "but God." Just so the purpose of negation of self is to clear the way for the apprehension of the fact that there is no existence but The One. The intoxication of life and its pleasures and occupations veils the Truth from men's eyes, and they ought to pass on to the spiritual intoxication which makes men beside themselves and lifts them to the beatific vision of eternal Truth. This is the same thing as saying they must pass on from negation to affirmation, from ignorance to the highest knowledge. This is illustrated by the story of the Turkish noble and the minstrel, which is given with an apology for using illustrations derived from drunkenness. A Turkish noble awoke from his drunken sleep, and called his minstrel to enliven him. The minstrel was a spiritual man, and proceeded to improve the occasion by singing a song with a deep spiritual meaning:
"I know not if thou art a moon or an idol,
I know not what thou requirest of me.
I know not what service to pay thee,
Whether to keep silence or to speak.
Thou art not apart from me, yet, strange to say,
I know not where I am, or where thou art.
I know not wherefore thou art dragging me,

Now embracing me, and now wounding me!"
Thus the whole of his song consisted of repetitions of the words, "I know not." At last the noble could endure it no longer, and he took a stick and threatened to beat the minstrel, saying, "O wretch, tell us something you do know, and do not repeat what you do not know. if I ask you whence you come or what you have eaten, and you answer only by negations, your answer is a waste of time. Say what you mean by all these negations." The minstrel replied, "My meaning is a concealed one. I fear to make affirmations in opposition to your negations, so I state negations that you may get a hint of the corresponding affirmations from them. I now hint the truth to you in my song; and when death comes to you, you will learn the mysteries which at present I can only hint."

Spiritual mysteries set forth in the Masnavi under similes of intoxication.

That wine of God is gained from that minstrel, 2
This bodily wine from this minstrel.
Both of these have one and the same name in speech,
But the difference between their worth is great.
Men's bodies are like pitchers with closed mouths;
Beware, till you see what is inside them.
The pitcher of this body holds the water of life,
Whilst that one holds deadly poison.
If you look at the contents you are wise;
If you look only at the vessel you are misguided.
Know words resemble these bodies,
And the meaning resembles the soul.
The body's eyes are ever intent on bodies,
The soul's eyes on the reasonable soul;
Wherefore, in the figures of the words of the Masnavi,
The form misleads, but the inner meaning guides.
In the Koran it is declared that its parables
"Mislead some and guide some." 3
O God! when a spiritual man talks of wine,
How can a fellow spiritual man mistake his meaning?
Thus that minstrel began his intoxicating song,

"O give me Thy cup, Thou whom I see not!
Thou art my face; what wonder if I see it not?
Extreme nearness acts as an obscuring veil. 4
Thou art my reason; what wonder if I see Thee not
Through the multitude of intervening obstacles?
Thou art 'nearer to me than my neck vein,' 5
How can I call to Thee, 'Ho,' as if thou wert far off?
Nay, but I will mislead some by calling in the desert,
To hide my Beloved from those of whom I am jealous!"
This is illustrated by an anecdote of the Prophet and Ayisha. Ayisha
was once sitting with the Prophet without her veil, when a blind
man came in. Ayisha, knowing well the jealous disposition of her
husband, at once prepared to retire on which the Prophet said,
"The man is blind and cannot see you." Ayisha replied by signs that
though the man could not see her she could see him. Just so the
spiritual man is jealous of exposing his mysteries to the gaze of the
profane, and from excess of caution veils them in signs and hints.
Then comes a commentary on the tradition, "Die before you die,"
i.e., mortify your carnal passions and lusts, and deny and annihilate
your carnal " self" before the death of the body overtakes you. Men
who put off repentance till they are at the point of death are
likened to the Shi'as of Aleppo, who every year on the Ashura, or
tenth day of Muharram, meet at the Antioch gate to bewail the
martyrdom of Hasan and Husain. Once, while they were thus
engaged, a Sunni poet arrived at the city, and inquired the reason of
this excessive grief and mourning. The Shi'as rebuked him for his
ignorance of sacred history, and he said, "This martyrdom
happened a long time ago; but it would seem, from your excessive
grief, that the news of it has only just reached you. You must have
been sleeping all this time not to have heard it before, and now you
are mourning for your own sleepiness!" To the truly spiritual, who
have drunk of God's wine and bear the "tokens of it on their
foreheads," 6 death is an occasion for rejoicing, not for wailing. The
man who is engrossed with the trifling pleasures of the world and
blind to the ample provision made for the soul is like an ant in a
barn of wheat, toiling to carry off a single grain, when ample stores

of wheat are already at its disposal. Spiritual men must continue urging the worldly to repent and avail themselves of this heavenly provision for their souls, careless, like Noah, whether their preaching is listened to or not. This is illustrated by an anecdote of a man who knocked at the door of an empty house at midnight, in order to give notice that it was time to prepare the meal taken at dawn in Ramazan.

Reason for knocking at the empty house.

You have said your say; now hear my answer,
So as not to remain in astonishment and bewilderment.
Though to you this time seems midnight,
To me the dawn of joyful morn seems nigh.
To the vulgar all parts of the world seem dead,
But to God they are instinct with sense and love.
And as to your saying that "this house is empty,
Why then should I beat a drum before it?"
Know that the people of God expend money,
And build many mosques and holy places,
And spend health and wealth in distant pilgrimages,
In ecstatic delight, like intoxicated lovers;
And none of them ever say, "The Ka'ba is empty;"
How can one who knows the truth say that?
These people are ranged in battle array,
And risk their lives to gain God's favor;
One plunged in calamities like Job himself,
Another exhibiting patience like Jacob.
Thousands of them are thirsty and afflicted,
Striving in earnest desire to do God's will.
I likewise, in order to please the merciful God,
Beat my drum at every door in hope of dawn.
Seek ye a purchaser who will pay you gold;
Where will you find one more liberal than God?
He buys the worthless rubbish which is your wealth,
He pays you the light that illumines your heart.
He accepts these frozen and lifeless bodies of yours,
And gives you a kingdom beyond what you dream of.

16

He takes a few drops of your tears,
And gives you the divine fount sweeter than sugar.
He takes your sighs fraught with grief and sadness,
And for each sigh gives rank in heaven as interest.
In return for the sigh-wind that raised tear-clouds,
God gave Abraham the title of "Father of the faithful."
Come! in this incomparable and crowded mart
Sell your old goods and take a kingdom in payment!

*NOTES:

1. Koran cxii. 4.

2. "A wine cup tempered at the camphor fountain shall the just quaff" (Koran lxxvi. 5).

3. Koran ii. 24.

4. See couplet 122 of the Guishan i Raz:

"When the object looked at is very close to the eye,
The eye is darkened so that it cannot see it."

I.e., When man is united with God he can no longer behold Him, for he is dwelling in Him.

5. Koran l. 15.

6. Koran xlviii. 29.

STORY IV.

The Purchase of Bilal.
To illustrate the rich recompense that is awarded to those who are
faithful in tribulation, the story of Bilal is next recounted at length.
Bilal was an Abyssinian slave belonging to a Jew of Mecca, and had
incurred his master's displeasure in consequence of having
embraced Islam. For this offence his master tortured him by
exposing him to the heat of the midday sun, and beating him with
thorns. But notwithstanding his anguish, Bilal would not recant his
faith, and uttered only the cry, "Ahad, Ahad!" "The One, the One
God!" At this moment Abu Bakr, the "Faithful witness," happened
to pass by, and was so struck by his constancy that he resolved to
buy him of the Jew. After much higgling and attempts at cheating
on the Jew's part he succeeded in doing so, and at once set him
free. When the Prophet heard of this purchase he said to Abu Bakr,
"Give me a share in him;" but Abu Bakr told him, somewhat to his
annoyance, that he had already set him free. Notwithstanding this
Bilal attached himself to the Prophet, and was afterwards
promoted to the honourable post of the Prophet's Mu'azzin.
This is followed by the story of Hilal, another holy man who, like
Bilal and Luqman and Joseph, served a noble in the capacity of
groom. His affections were set on things above, and he was ever
pressing upwards towards the high mark of spiritual exaltation, and
saying, like Moses, "I will not stop till I reach the confluence of the
two seas, and for years will I journey on." 1 Herein he presented a
great contrast to ordinary men, who are ever giving way to their
lusts, and so being dragged down into the state of mere animals, or
even lower. Hilal's master was a Mosalman, yet one whose eyes
were only partially open to the truth. He was in the habit of asking
his guests their age; and if they answered doubtfully, saying,
"Perhaps eighteen, or seventeen, or sixteen, or even fifteen," he

would rebuke them, saying, "As you seem to be putting yourself lower and lower, you had better go back at once to your mother's womb." These guests are a type of men who lower themselves from the rank of humanity to that of animals. This master, however, was blind to Hilal's spiritual excellence, and allowed him to drag on a miserable existence in his stables. At last Hilal fell sick; but no one cared for him, till the Prophet himself, warned by a divine intimation, came to visit him, and commiserated his wretched condition. Hilal proved himself to be faithful through tribulation; for, instead of grumbling at his lot, he replied, "How is that sleep wretched which is broken by the advent of the Sun of prophecy? or how can he be called athirst on whose head is poured the water of life?" In truth, Hilal had by degrees become purified from the stain of earthly existence and earthly qualities, and washed in the fountain of the water of life, i.e., the holy revelations of the Prophet, till he had attained the exalted grade of purity enjoined on those who would study God's Word aright. 2

Growth in grace is accomplished by slow degrees, and not per saltum.

Since you have told the story of Hilal (the new moon)
Now set forth the story of Badr (the full moon).
That new moon and that full moon are now united,
Removed from duality and defect and shortcomings.
That Hilal is now exalted above inward defect;
His outward defects served as degrees of ascension.
Night after night that mentor taught him grades of ascent
And through his patient waiting gave him happiness.
The mentor says, "O raw hastener, through patient waiting,
You must climb to the summit step by step.
Boil your pot by degrees and in a masterly way;
Food boiled in mad haste is spoiled.
Doubtless God could have created the universe
By the fiat 'Be!' in one moment of time;
Why, then, did He protract His work over six days,
Each of which equaled a thousand years, O disciple?
Why does the formation of an infant take nine months?

Because God's method is to work by slow degrees,
Why did the formation of Adam take forty days?
Because his clay was kneaded by slow degrees.
Not hurrying on like you, O raw one,
Who claim to be a Shaikh whilst yet only a child!
You run up like a gourd higher than all plants,
But where is your power of resistance or combat?
You have leant on trees or on walls,
And so mounted up like a gourd, O little dog rose;
Even though your prop may be a lofty cypress,
At last you are seen to be dry and hollow.
O gourd, your bright green hue soon turns yellow.
For it is not a natural but an artificial color."
This is illustrated by an anecdote of an ugly old hag who painted her
face to make it look pretty, but was detected and exposed to scorn.
*NOTES:
1. Koran xviii. 59.
2. Koran lvi. 79.

STORY V.

The Sufi and the Qazi.
A sick man laboring under an incurable disease went to a physician for advice. The physician felt his pulse, and perceived that no treatment would cure him, and therefore told him to go away and do whatever he had a fancy for. This was the advice given by God to the Israelites when they were seen to be incurable by the admonitions of the prophets. "Do what you will, but God's eye is on all your doings." 1 The sick man blessed the physician for his agreeable prescription, and at once went to a stream, where he saw a Sufi bathing his feet. He was seized with a desire to hit the Sufi on the back, and, calling to mind the physician's advice, at once carried his wish into effect. The Sufi jumped up, and was about to return the blow, but when he saw the weakly and infirm condition of his assailant he restrained himself. He disregarded his present angry impulse, and had regard to the future, so that the non-existent future became to him more really existent than the existing present. Here the poet digresses to point out that when wise men recognize the true relative importance of the present and the future they cease to shrink from death and annihilation, which lifts them to a higher and nobler life. This is illustrated by an anecdote of Mahmud of Ghazni, quoted from Faridu- 'd-Din 'Attar. Mahmud, in one of his campaigns, took prisoner a Hindu boy, who at first regarded him with the greatest dread, in consequence of the stories he had heard of him from his mother, but afterwards experienced Mahmud's kindness and tenderness, and came to know him and love him. So it is with death. According to the Hadis "Those who have passed away do not grieve because of death, but because of wasted opportunities in life." The Masnavi is "a shop of poverty and self-abnegation," and a treasury containing only the doctrines of "Unity;" and if its stories suggest aught else, that is due to the evil

promptings of Iblis, who also misled the Prophet himself to attribute undue power to the idols Lat and 'Uzza and Manat, in a verse which was afterwards cancelled. 2 The Sufi, being full of the spirit of self-abnegation, did not retaliate on his weak, assailant but led him before the Qazi. On learning the facts of the case the Qazi said, "This Faqir is sick to death, and you, being a Sufi, are, according to your profession, dead to the world. How, then, can I award a penalty against him in your favor? I am a judge, not of the dead, but of the living." The Sufi was dissatisfied with this view of the case, and again pressed the Qazi to do him justice. On this the Qazi asked the sick Faqir how much money he had, and on his replying, "Six dirhams," took pity on him, and let him off with a fine of three dirhams only. The moment the sentence was pronounced the sick Faqir went up to the Qazi and struck him a blow on the back, and cried out, "Now take the other three dirhams and let me go!" The Sufi then pointed out to the Qazi that by his ill-timed leniency to the Faqir he had brought this blow upon himself, and urged him to apply in his own case those principles of mercy and forgiveness which he had proposed in the case of another. The Qazi said that, for his part, he recognized every blow and misfortune that might befall him as divinely ordained, and sent for his good, according to the text, "Laugh little and weep much," 3 and that his judgment in the matter of the Faqir had not been dictated by impulse, but by inspiration. 4 The Sufi again asked him how evils and misfortunes could proceed from the divine fount of good, and the Qazi replied that what seems good and evil to us has no absolute existence, but is merely as the foam on the surface of the vast ocean. Moreover, every misfortune occurring to the faithful in this life will be amply compensated for in the life to come. The Sufi asked why this world should not be so arranged that only good should be experienced in it, and the Qazi replied by telling him an anecdote of a Turk and a tailor. The Turk, who typifies the careless pleasure-seeker, was so intent on listening to the jokes and amusing stories of the tailor, typifying the seductive world, that he allowed himself to be robbed of the silk which was to furnish him with a vesture for eternity. The Sufi again retorted that he did not see why the world would not get on better without the evil in it, and the Qazi replied with the poet's favorite argument that there would be no possibility of being virtuous if there were no temptations to be vicious. As Bishop Butler says, this life is a state of probation, and such a state necessarily involves trials and difficulties and dangers to be resisted and overcome.

The dead regret not dying, but having lost opportunities in life.
Well said that Leader of mankind,
That whosoever passes away from the world
Does not grieve and lament over his death,
But grieves ever over lost opportunities.
He says, "Why did I not keep death always in view,
Which is the treasury of wealth and sustenance?
Why did I blindly all my life set my affections
On vain shadows which perish at death?
My regret is not that I have died,
But that I rested on these vain shadows in life.
I saw not that my body was a mere shadow or foam,
Which foam rises out of and lives on the Ocean (God).
When the Ocean casts its foam-drops to land,
Go to the graveyard and behold them,
And ask them, "Where is your motion and activity?
The Ocean has cast you into a mortal sickness!"
They will answer by their condition, if not with words,
"Put this question to the Ocean, not to us!"
How can mere foam move unless moved by the waves?
How can dust mount on high unless raised by wind?
When you see the dust-cloud, see the wind too!
When you see the foam, see the ocean that heaves it!
Ah! look till you see your own real final cause,
The rest of you is only fat and flesh, warp and woof.
Your fat kindles no light or flame in a lamp;
Your kneaded flesh is not good for roasting.
Burn up, then, all this body of yours with discernment;
Rise to sight, to sight, to sight!
Virtue cannot exist without temptation and difficulties to be

overcome.
The Sufi said, "The Great Helper is able
To procure for us profit without loss.
He who casts into the fire roses and trees
Can accomplish good without injury to any.
He who extracts the rose from the thorn
Can also turn this winter into spring.
He who exalts the heads of the cypresses
Is able also out of sadness to bring joy.
He by whose fiat all non-existent things exist,
What harm to Him were it if He made them eternal?
He who gave to the body a soul and made it live,
What loss to Him were it if He never caused it to die?
How would it be if That Liberal One were to give
Their hearts' desire to his slaves without toil,
And keep away from these feeble ones
The ambushed snares of lust and temptations of Iblis?"
The Qazi said, "If there were no bitter things,
And no opposition of fair and foul, stone and pearl,
And no lust or Satan or concupiscence,
And no wounds or war or fraud,
Pray, O destroyer of virtue, by what name and title
Could the King of kings address His slaves?
How could He say, 'O temperate or O meek one!'
Or, 'O courageous one, or O wise one?'
How could there be temperate, gentle, or liberal men
If there were no cursed Satan to tempt them astray?
Rustam and Hamza would be all the same as cowards;
Wisdom and knowledge would be useless and vain.
Wisdom and knowledge serve to guide the wanderers;
Were there but one road wisdom would be needless.
To pamper the house of your body fleeting as water,
Do you think it right to ruin both worlds?
I know you are pure of guile and ripe,
And ask this only to edify the ignorant.
The ills of fortune and all troubles soever

Are better than exile from God and neglect of Him;
For the former pass away, but the latter abide;
He is happy who carries a wary heart before God." 5
This is illustrated by an anecdote of a woman who complained of
the hard life she had to lead with her husband owing to his poverty,
and was silenced by being asked whether she would prefer to be
divorced. No troubles are so hard to hear as separation from the
Beloved. Fasting and holy war bring pains with them, but not so
great as those incurred by banishment from God. In the midst of
their troubles God is ever caring for His servants, and they must not
let their tribulations blot out the memory of God's previous
goodness to them.
To do this shows an entire absence of growth in grace. This is
illustrated by an anecdote of a sage and a monk. The sage asked the
monk which was the older, his white beard or himself. The monk
replied that he himself was older by some years, whereupon the
sage rebuked him for his ignorance, saying his beard had grown
pure and white, but he was still black with sin, and had progressed
not at all in goodness since he was born.
Each of our members testifies to God's bounties towards us.
Inquire now, I pray, of each one of your members;
These dumb members have a thousand tongues.
Inquire the detail of the bounties of the All-sustainer,
Which are recorded in the volume of the universe.
Day and night you are eagerly asking for news,
Whilst every member of your body is telling you news.
Since each member of your body issued from Not-being,
How much pleasure has it seen, and how much pain?
For no member grows and flourishes without pleasure,
And each member is weakened by every pain. 6
The member endures, but that pleasure is forgotten,
Yet not all forgotten, but hidden from the senses.
Like summer wherein cotton is produced,
The cotton remains, but the summer is forgotten.
Or like ice which is formed in great frost,
The frost departs, but the ice is still before us.

The ice is mindful of that extreme cold,
And even in winter that crop is mindful of the summer.
In like manner, O son, every member of your body
Tells you tales of God's bounties to your body.
Even as a woman who has borne twenty children,
Each child tells a tale of pleasure felt by her.
She became not pregnant save after sexual pleasure,
Can a garden bloom without the spring?
Pregnant women and their teeming wombs
Tell tales of love frolics in the spring.
So every tree which nurtures its fruits
Has been, like Mary, impregnated by the Unseen King.
Though fire's heat be hidden in the midst of water,
Yet a thousand boiling bubbles prove it present.
Though the heat of the fire be working unseen,
Yet its bubbles signify its presence plainly.
In like manner, the members of those enjoying "union"
Become big with child, viz., with forms of "states" and "words." 7
Gazing on the beauty of these forms they stand agape,
And the forms of the world vanish from their sight.
These spiritual progenies are not born of the elements,
And are perforce invisible to the sensual eye.
These progenies are born of divine apparitions,
And are therefore bidden by veils without color.
I said "born," but in reality they are not born;
I used this expression only by way of indication.
But keep silence till the King bids you speak,
Offer not your nightingale songs to these roses;
For they themselves are saying to you in loud tones,
"O nightingale, hold your peace, and listen to us!"
Those two kinds of fair forms (ecstatic states and words)
Are undeniable proofs of a previous "union;"
Yea, those two kinds of exalted manifestations
Are the evident fruits of a preceding wedlock.
The ecstasy is past, but your members recall it;
Ask them about it, or call it to mind yourself.

When sorrow seizes you, if you are wise,
You will question that sorrow-fraught moment,
Saying to it, "O sorrow, who now deniest
Thy portion of bounty given thee by the Perfect One,
Even if each moment be not to thee a glad spring,
Yet of what is thy body, like a rose-heap, a storehouse?
Thy body is a heap of roses, thy thought rosewater;
'Twere strange if rosewater ignored the rose-heap!"

*NOTES:

1. Koran xli. 40.
2. Koran liii. 19, and Rodwell's note.
3. Koran ix. 84.
4. Koran liii. 3.
5. Koran xxvi. 88.
6. Cp. Nicom. Ethics, x., iv. 6.
7. Compare Gulshan i Raz, I. 624. Ecstatic words and states are the offspring of communion with God.

STORY VI.

The Faqir and the Hidden Treasure.
Notwithstanding the clear evidence of God's bounty, engendering
these spiritual states in men, philosophers and learned men, wise in
their own conceit, obstinately shut their eyes to it, and look afar off
for what is really close to them, so that they incur the penalty of
"being branded on the nostrils," 1 adjudged against unbelievers.
This is illustrated by the story of a poor Faqir who prayed to God
that he might be fed without being obliged to work for his food. A
divine voice came to him in his sleep and directed him to go to the
house of a certain scribe and take a certain writing that he should
find there. He did so, and on reading the writing found that it
contained directions for finding a hidden treasure. The directions
were as follows: "Go outside the city to the dome which covers the
tomb of the martyr; turn your back to the tomb and your face
towards Mecca, place an arrow in your bow, and where the arrow
falls there dig for the treasure." But before the Faqir had time to
commence the search the rumor of the writing and its contents had
reached the king, who at once sent and took it away from the Faqir,
and began to search for the treasure on his own account. After
shooting many arrows and digging in all directions the king failed to
find the treasure, and got weary of searching, and returned the
writing to the Faqir. Then the Faqir tried what he could do, but
failed altogether to hit the spot where the treasure was buried. At
last, despairing of success by his own unaided efforts, he cast his
care upon God, and implored the divine assistance. Then a voice
from heaven came to him, saying, "You were directed to fix an
arrow on your bow, but not to draw your bow with all your might,
as you have been doing. Shoot as gently as possible, that the arrow
may fall close to you, for the hidden treasure is indeed 'nearer to
you than your neck-vein.' "2 Men overlook the spiritual treasures

close to them, and for this reason it is that prophets have no honor
in their own countries, as is illustrated by the cases of the saint Abu-
'l-Hasan Khirqani and the Prophet Hud or Heber.
God rules men by alternations of hope and fear.
This sad Faqir too put up his cries for aid,
And bore off the ball of acceptance from the field.
But at times he distrusted the efficacy of his prayers,
On account of the delay in answering them.
Again, hope of the mercy of the Lord
Arose in his heart as an earnest of rejoicing.
When he was hopeless and ceasing to pray in weariness
He heard from God the word "Ascend!"
God is an Abaser and an Exalter
Without these two processes nothing comes into being.
Behold the abasement of earth and uplifting of heaven;
Without these two heaven would not revolve, O man!
The abasement and exaltation of earth is otherwise,
Half the year is barren, half green and verdant.
The abasement and exaltation of weary time
Is otherwise again, half day and half night.
The abasement and exaltation of this compound body
Is now health and now grievous sickness.
Know all the conditions of the world are in this wise,
Drought, famine, peace, war, and trials.
This world flies, as it were, with these two wings;
Through these all souls are homes of hope and fear;
So that the world keeps trembling like leaves,
In the cold and hot winds of death and resurrection.
Till tbe jar of pure wine of our 'Isa (Unity)
Shall supersede the jar of many-colored wine (plurality),
For that world (of unity) is as a saltpan;
Whatever enters it loses its varied hues.
On the text, "Verily I am about to place a Khalifa or Vicegerent on
earth" 3.
Whereas the aim and will of the Merciful God
Inclined to the revelation and manifestation of Himself,

And one opposite cannot be shown but by its opposite,
And that Unique King of kings has no opposite or peer, 4
Therefore that Lord of the heart set up a Khalifa,
To serve as a mirror to reflect His own sovereignty.
Therefore He gave him unlimited purity and light,
And on the other side He set darkness opposing the light. 5
God set up two standards, a white and a black one,
The one Adam and the other Iblis;
And between these two mighty armies
Ensued war and battle and all we have witnessed.
Thus, too, in the second generation lived pure Abel;
Cain was the opposite of his pure light.
In like manner these two standards of right and wrong
Were borne aloft till the age of Nimrod.
Nimrod was the opponent and adversary of Abraham,
And their opposing camps warred and fought one another.
When God grew weary of the length of this war,
His fire was appointed to arbitrate between them.
He commanded fire and its flaming torment
To settle the matter in dispute between them.
Age after age these two parties contended,
Even till the time of Pharaoh and gentle Moses.
Between these two the war was waged for years,
And when it passed all bounds and affliction increased
God made the water of the Nile a judge between them,
That the one who deserved preeminence should endure.
In like manner it went on till the time of Mustafa
And Abu Jahl, that prince of iniquity.
Likewise did God ordain a punishment for the Thamud,
Namely, an earthquake which destroyed their lives.
Likewise a punishment for the Adites,
Namely, a swiftly rising and violent wind.
Likewise God ordained acute punishment for Qarun;
For the earth concealed wrath under its mildness,
Till all its mildness was converted into wrath,
And it swallowed up Qarun and his wealth in its depth.

So with the mouthful which nourishes your body
And wards off the darts of hunger like a cuirass,
When God instils wrath into this mouthful of bread,
That same bread will choke you like a halter.
This same garment which protects you from the cold,
God may give it the quality of intense cold,
So that this warm vest may become to your body
Cold as ice and biting as frost;
So that you will cast off these furs and silks,
And seek for a refuge from cold with cold itself.
You have only one eye, not two (for these two possibilities).
You have forgotten the story of the "shadowing cloud." 6
God's command came to city and village,
And to house and wall, saying, "Afford no shade!
Ward not off the pouring rain and the sun's heat;"
Till those men hasted to listen to the prophet Shu'aib,
Saying, 'O king, have pity; most of us are dead!'
But read the rest of the tale in the commentaries.
When that Omnipotent hand made the staff a serpent,
If you have reason, that portent should suffice.
You have sight indeed, but fail to mark carefully;
Your eyes are dimmed and closed with fat.
The heavenly treasure lies "nearer to us than our neck-vein".
The Faqir was in this state when a divine voice came,
And God thus solved his difficulties,
Saying, "The voice told you to place an arrow on the bow,
It did not bid you draw the bowstring to the utmost;
It did not bid you draw the bow with all your might;
It said, 'Adjust an arrow,' not 'Draw the bow fully.'
You elevated the bow to excess,
You magnified unduly the bowman's art,
Go! abandon this strong bowmanship,
Fix an arrow on the string, but make it not fly far.
When it falls, dig in that spot and search,
Abandon force and seek the treasure with humility."
God is "what is nearer to you than your neck-vein,"

You have cast the arrow of speculation afar off.
O you, who have made ready your bow and arrows,
The game is close to you, and you shoot too far off.
The further a man shoots, the further off he is,
And the more removed from the treasure he seeks.
The philosopher kills himself with thinking,
Tell him that his back is turned to that treasure;
Tell him that the more he runs to and fro,
The Almighty says, "Make efforts in our ways," 7
Not "Make efforts away from us," O restless one.
Like Canaan, who went away, from shame to follow Noah,
Up to the top of that lofty mountain,
The more he sought safety on that mountain,
The further was he removed from the safe asylum.
So this Faqir, in search of that hidden treasure,
Day after day drew his bow stronger and stronger;
And the harder he drew his bow,
The further was he from the seat of that treasure.
This parable applies to all times,
For the soul of the ignorant is pledged to misfortune.
Because the ignorant man is ashamed of a master,
Perforce he goes and opens a new school for himself.
That school is higher than your true master, O beloved,
And hard of access, and full of scorpions and snakes.
Straightway overthrow it, and turn back again
To the green garden and sweet watered meadows.
Not like Canaan, who, through pride and ignorance,
Sought his ark of safety on a protecting mountain.
His far-shooting learning veiled his eyes,
While his heart's desire was all the while in his grasp.
Ah! oftentimes have learning and genius and wit
Proved to the traveler to be Ghouls and highwaymen!
"The majority of those in Paradise are the simple," 8
Who have escaped the snares of philosophy.
Strip yourself bare of overweening intellect,
That grace may ever be shed upon you from above.

Cleverness is the opposite of humility and submission,
Quit cleverness, and consort with simple-mindedness!
*NOTES:
1. Koran lxviii. 16.
2. Koran l. 15.
3. Koran ii. 28.
4. Because, as Sir T. Browne says, "God is all things."
5. See Gulshan i Raz, I. 265, and note.
6. Koran xxvi. 189. The cloud emitted heat instead of rain, to punish those who disregarded Shu'aib, or Jethro.
7. Koran xxix. 69.
8. A Hadis. Cp. 1 Cor. i. 25, 26.

STORY VII.

The Three Travelers.
A Mosalman was traveling with two unbelievers, a Jew and a
Christian. Like wisdom linked with the flesh and the devil. God was
"nigh unto His faithful servant," 1 and when the first stage was
completed He caused a present of sweetmeats to be laid before the
travelers. As the Jew and the Christian had already eaten their
evening meal when the sweetmeats arrived, they proposed to lay
them aside till the morrow; but the Mosalman, who was keeping
fast, and therefore could not eat before nightfall, proposed to eat
them that night. To this the other two refused to consent, alleging
that the Mosalman wanted to eat the whole of the sweetmeats
himself. Then the Mosalman proposed to divide them into three
portions, so that each might eat his own portion when he pleased;
but this also was objected to by the others, who quoted the
proverb, "The divider is in hell" The Mosalman explained to them
that this proverb meant the man who divides his allegiance
between God and lust; but they still refused to give way, and the
Mosalman therefore submitted, and lay down to sleep in the
endurance of the pangs of hunger. Next morning, when they
awoke, it was agreed between them that each should relate his
dreams, and that the sweetmeats should be awarded to him whose
dream was the best. The Jew said that he had dreamed that Moses
had carried him to the top of Mount Sinai, and shown him
marvelous visions of the glory of heaven and the angels. The
Christian said he had dreamed that 'Isa had carried him up to the
fourth heaven and shown him all the glories of the heavens. Finally
the Mosalman said that the Prophet Muhammad had appeared to
him in person, and after commending him for his piety in saying his
prayers and keeping fast so strictly on the previous night, had
commanded him to eat up those divinely provided sweetmeats as a

reward, and he had accordingly done so. The Jew and the Christian were at first annoyed with him for thus stealing a march upon them; but on his pointing out that he had no option but to obey the Prophet's commands, they admitted that he had done right, and that his dream was the best, as he had been awake, while they were asleep. The moral is, that the divine treasure is revealed as an immediate intuition to those who seek it with prayer and humble obedience, and not to those who seek to infer and deduce its nature and quality from the lofty abstractions of philosophy. Lofty philosophical speculation does not lead to the knowledge of God.

The Mosalman said, "O my friends,
My lord, the Prophet Muhammad, appeared to me
And said, 'The Jew has hurried to the top of Sinai,
And plays a game of love with God's interlocutor;
The Christian has been carried by 'Isa, Lord of bliss
Up to the summit of the fourth heaven
Thou who art left behind and hast endured anguish,
Arise quickly and eat the sweetmeats and confections!
Those two clever and learned men have ascended,
And read their titles of dignity and exaltation;
Those two exalted ones have found exalted science,
And rivaled the very angels in intellect;
O humble and simple and despised one,
Arise and eat of the banquet of the divine sweets!"
They said to him, "Then you have been gluttonous;
Well indeed! you have eaten all the sweets!"
He answered, "When my sovereign lord commanded me,
Who am I that I should abstain from obeying?
Would you, O Jew, resist the commands of Moses
If he bade you do something, either pleasant or not?
Would you, O Christian, rebel against 'Isa's commands,
Whether those commands were agreeable or the reverse?
How could I rebel against the 'Glory of the prophets'?
Nay, I ate the sweets, and am now happy."
They replied, "By Allah, you have seen a true vision;

Your vision is better than a hundred like ours.
Your dream was seen by you when awake, O happy one,
For it was seen to be real by your being awake."
Quit excessive speculation and inordinate science,
'Tis service of God and good conduct that gains its end.
'Tis for this that God created us,
"We created not mankind save to worship us" 2
What profit did his science bring to Samiri? 3
His science excluded him from God's portals.
Consider what Qarun gained by his alchemy;
He was swallowed up in the depths of the earth.
Abu-l Jahl, again, what gained he from his wit
Save to be hurled head-foremost into hell for infidelity?
Know real science is seeing the fire directly,
Not mere talk, inferring the fire from the smoke.
Your scientific proofs are more offensive to the wise
Than the urine and breath whence a physician infers.
If these be your only proofs, O son,
Smell foul breath and inspect urine like physicians.
Such proofs are as the staff of a blind man,
Which prove only the blindness of the holder.
All your outcry and pompous claims and bustle
Only say, "I cannot see, hold me excused!"

This is illustrated be an anecdote of a peasant who, hearing a proclamation issued by the Prince of Tirmid, to the effect that a large reward would be given to him who should take a message to Samarcaud in the space of four days, hurried to Tirmid by relays of post-horses in the utmost haste, and threw the whole city into alarm, as the people thought that his extreme haste and bustle must portend the approach of an enemy or some other calamity. But when he was admitted to the presence of the prince, all he had to say was, that he had hurried to inform him that he could not go to Samarcand so quickly. The prince was very angry with him for making all this disturbance about nothing, and threatened to punish him.

The uses of chastisements.

He said, "Alms of mercy repel calamity, 4
Alms cure thy sickness, O son
'Tis not charitable to burn up the poor,
Or to put out the eyes of the meek."
The prince replied, "Kindness is good in its place,
Provided you do kindness in its proper place.
If at chess you put the king in the rook's place
That is wrong; and so if you put the knight in the king's,
The law prescribes both rewards and chastisements.
The king's place is the throne, the horse's the gate.
What is justice but putting each in his place?
What injustice but putting each in what is not his place?
Nothing is vain of all that God has created,
Whether vengeance or mercy, or plain dealing or snares.
Not one of all these is good absolutely,
Nor is any one of them absolutely bad.
Each is harmful or beneficial according to its place,
Wherefore knowledge of these points is proper and useful.
Ah! many are the chastisements sent to the poor
Which are more beneficial to him than bread and sweets;
Because sweets out of season excite biliousness,
While blows make him pure from impurity.
Strike the poor man timely blows,
Which may save him from being beheaded later."
The peasant, in reply, urged the prince not to be over hasty in
punishing him, but to take counsel with suitable advisers, as
enjoined in various texts, 5 and in the Hadis prohibiting monkery,
and warned him that if he shunned the advice and society of his
equals he would assuredly be led astray by wretched companions. 6
In illustration of this a story is told of a mouse who conceived a
great affection for a frog living in a neighboring pond. 7 That he
might be able to communicate with his friend at all times, he
fastened a string to the frog's leg, and the other end of it to his own.
The proverb says, "Occasional intermission of visits augments love,"
8 but ardent lovers desire to be in communication with the object
of their love without intermission. The frog was at first unwilling to

enter into such close relations with an animal of another species, but at last allowed himself to be persuaded to do so, against his better judgment. Shortly afterwards a raven swooped down on the mouse and carried him off, and the frog, being fastened to the mouse, was dragged off and destroyed along with it. The raven's friends said to him, "How is it you managed to catch an animal that lives in the water?" and he replied, "Because it was so silly as to consort with one of another species that lived on dry land."

Comparison of the body to the mouse, and the soul to the frog.
The two friends discussed the matter long,
And after discussion this plan was settled,
That they should fetch a long string,
By means of which to communicate with one another.
The mouse said, "One end must be tied to your leg,
And the other end to the leg of me, your double,
That by this contrivance we two may be united,
And be mingled together like soul and body."
Body is like a string tied to sod's foot,
That string drags soul down to earth.
The soul is the frog in the water of ecstatic bliss;
Escaping from the mouse of the body, it is in bliss.
The mouse of the body drags it back with that string;
Ah! what sorrow it tastes through being dragged back
If it were not dragged down by that insolent mouse,
The frog would remain at peace in its water.
On the last day, when you shall awake from sleep,
You will learn the rest of this from the Sun of truth!

In illustration of the thesis that the sense which perceives the unseen and spiritual world is superior to the other senses, and is exempt from death and decay, the poet tells an anecdote of Sultan Mahmud of Ghazni and some robbers. One night, when walking about the city alone, he fell in with a band of robbers. He told them he was one of them, and proposed that each should tell his own special talent. Accordingly one said he could hear what the dogs said when they barked; another that his sight was so good that when he saw a man at night he could recognize him without fail next day; another said his talent lay in the strength of his arms, whereby he dug holes through the walls of houses another said he could divine by his sense of smell where gold was hidden; another said his wrist was so strong that he could throw a rope farther than any one. At last it came to the turn of the king, and he told them that his talent lay in his beard, for when he wagged it he could deliver criminals from the executioner. The robbers then went to the king's palace, and, each of them co-operating by the exercise of his peculiar talent, they broke into it, and plundered a large sum of money. The king, after witnessing the burglary, withdrew from them secretly, and, having summoned his Vazir, gave orders for their apprehension. No sooner were the robbers brought before the king than the one whose talent lay in recognizing by day those whom he had seen in the darkness of night at once knew him, and said to the others, "This is the man who said his talent lay in his beard!" Thus the only one whose talent profited him at the time of need was he who could recognize by day what he had previously seen by night; for he appealed to the king to exercise his talent of deliverance, and the king listened to his entreaty, and delivered him from the executioner.

He whose eyes discern God in the world is safe from destruction.
He who, when he had once seen a person at night,
Recognized him without fail when he saw him by day,
Saw the king upon the throne, and straightway cried,
"This was he who accompanied us on our nightly walk;
This is he whose beard possessed such rare talent;
Our arrest is due to his sagacity."
He added, "'Yea, he was with you,' 9 this great king;
He beheld our actions and heard our secrets.
My eyes guided me to recognize that king at night,
And dwelt lovingly on his face, like the moon at night.
Now, therefore, I will implore his grace for myself,
For he will never avert his face from him that knew him."
Know the eye of the ' Knower is a safeguard in both worlds,
For therein ye will find a very Bahram to aid you.
For this cause Muhammad was the intercessor for faults,

Because his eye 'did not wander' 10 from the King of kings.
In the night of this world, when the sun is hidden,
He beheld God, and placed his hopes on Him.
His eyes were anointed with the words, ' We opened thy heart,' 11
He beheld what Gabriel himself had not power to see." 12
The story of the frog is concluded by the lamentations of the frog
over his folly in consorting with an animal of a different genus to his
own, on which Reason warns him that homogeneity lies in spirit,
not in outward form; and this is illustrated by an anecdote of a man
named 'Abdu'l Ghaus, who was the son of a fairy mother, and
consequently homogeneous with the fairies, though only an
ordinary man to outward appearance.

*NOTES:

1. Koran ii. 182.
2. Koran ii. 56.
3. Samiri, the maker of the golden calf. Qarun Korah.
4. Freytag Arabum Proverbia, iii. 277.
5. Koran lxvii. 22, iii. 155, xlii. 36.
6. Koran xliii. 37.
7. Anvari Suhaili, Chap. vii. Story III.
8. Freytag, Arabum Proverbia, i. 287.
9. Koran lvii. 4.
10. Koran liii. 17.
11. Koran xciv. 1.
12. Gulshan i Raz, I. 120.

STORY VIII.

The Man who received a Pension from the Prefect of Tabriz.
These reflections on the nothingness of outward form compared to
spirit lead the poet to the corollary that often men whose outward
forms are buried in the grave are greater benefactors to the poor
and helpless than men still living in the body. This is illustrated by
the story of the man who was maintained by the Prefect of Tabriz.
This man incurred heavy debts on the credit of his pension, even as
the Imam Ja'far Sadiq was able to capture a strong fort single-
handed through the power of God assisting him. When the
creditors became pressing the man journeyed to Tabriz to seek
further aid; but on arriving there he found the Prefect was dead. On
learning this he was much cast down, but eventually recognized
that he had erred in looking to a creature instead of his Creator for
aid, according to the text, "The infidels equalize others with their
Lord." 1 This obliquity of spiritual sight, causing him to see a mere
human benefactor, where the real benefactor was God alone, is
illustrated by anecdotes of a man buying bread at Kashan, of Sultan
Khwarazm Shah deluded into disliking a fine horse by the interested
advice of his Vazir, and of Joseph, who when imprisoned by
Pharaoh was induced to trust for deliverance to the intercession of
the chief butler rather than to God alone, for which cause "he
remained several years in prison." 2 A charitable person of Tabriz
endeavoured to raise funds for the poor man, and appealed to the
citizens to aid him, but only succeeded in collecting a very small
sum. He then visited the Prefect's tomb, and implored assistance
from him; and the same night the Prefect appeared to him in a
dream, and gave him directions where to find a great treasure, and
directed him to make over this treasure to the poor man. Thus the
dead Prefect proved a more liberal benefactor than the citizens of
Tabriz who were still living.

The poor man's regrets for having placed his trust in man and not in God.

When he recovered himself he said, "O God,
I have sinned in looking for aid to a creature!
Although the Prefect showed great liberality,
It was in no wise equal to Thy bounty.
He gave me a cap, but Thou my head full of sense;
He gave me a garment, but Thou my tall form.
He gave me gold, but Thou my hand which counts it;
He gave me a horse, but Thou my reason to guide it;
He gave me a lamp, but Thou my lucid eyes;
He gave me sweetmeats, but Thou my appetite for them;
He gave me a pension, but Thou my life and being;
His gift was gold, but Thine true blessings;
He gave me a house, but Thou heaven and earth;
In Thy house he and a hundred like him are nourished.
The gold was of Thy providing, he did not create it;
The bread of Thy providing, and furnished to him by Thee.
Thou also didst give him his liberality,
For thereby Thou didst augment his happiness.
I made him my Qibla, and directed my prayers to him;
I turned away my eyes from Thee, the Qibla-maker!
Where was he when the Supreme Dispenser of faith
Sowed reason in the water and clay of man,
And drew forth from Not-being this heavenly dome,
And spread out the carpet of the earth?
Of the stars He made torches to illumine the sky,
And of the four elements locks with keys (of reason).
Ah! many are the buildings visible and invisible
Which God has made between heaven's dome and earth.
Man is the astrolabe of those exalted attributes,
The attribute of man is to manifest God's signs.
Whatever is seen in man is the reflection of God,
Even as the reflection of the moon in water."
Say not two, know not two, call not on two!
Know the slave is obliterated in his lord!

So the lord is obliterated in God that created him
Yea, lost and dead and buried in his Creator!
When you regard this lord as separate from God,
You annihilate at once text and paraphrase.
With eyes and heart look beyond mere water and clay,
God alone is the Qibla; regard not two Qiblas!
If you regard two you lose the benefit of both;
A spark falls on the tinder and the tinder vanishes!
Joseph kept in prison a long time for having placed his hopes of
release in man and not in God.
In like manner Joseph, in the prison,
With humble and earnest supplications
Begged aid, saying, "When you are released,
And are occupied with your ministrations to the king,
Remember me, and entreat the king
To release rue too from this prison."
How can one prisoner fettered in the snare
Procure release for a fellow prisoner?
The people of the world are all prisoners,
Awaiting death on the stake of annihilation;
Except one or two rare exceptions,
Whose bodies are in prison but their souls in heaven.
Afterwards, because Joseph had looked to man for aid,
He remained in prison for many years.
The Devil caused the man to forget Joseph,
And blotted Joseph's words from his remembrance;
And on account of this fault of that holy man
God left him in the prison for many years.
*NOTES:
1. Koran vi. 1.
2. Koran xii. 42.
3. Koran xii. 42.

STORY IX.

The King and his Three Sons.

A certain king had three sons, who were the light of his eyes, and, as it were, a fountain whence the palm tree of his heart drank the water of bliss. One day he called his sons before him and commanded them to travel through his realm, and to inspect the behavior of the governors and the state of the administration; and he strictly charged them not to go near a particular fort which he named. But, according to the saying, "Man hankers after what is forbidden," the three princes disobeyed their father, and, before going anywhere else, proceeded to visit this fort. The result was, that they fell into calamities, and had occasion to repeat the text, "Had we but hearkened or understood, we had not been among the dwellers in the flame." 1 The fort was full of pictures, images and forms, and amongst them was a portrait of a beautiful damsel, the daughter of the King of China, which made such a deep impression on the three princes that they all became distracted with love and determined to journey to the court of the King of China and sue for the hand of his daughter.

The significance of forms. 2

Be not intoxicated with these goblets of forms,
Lest you become a maker and worshipper of idols.
Pass by these cups full of forms, linger not;
There is wine in the cups, but it proceeds not from them.
Look to the Giver of the wine with open mouth;
When His wine comes, is not cup too small to hold it?
O Adam, seek the reality of my love,
Quit the mere husk and form of the wheat.
When sand was made meal for "The Friend of God," 3
Know, O master, the form of wheat was dispensed with.
Form proceeds from the world that is without form,
Even as smoke arises from fire.
The Divine art without form designs forms (ideals), 4
Those forms fashion bodies with senses and instruments.
Whatever the form, it fashions in its own likeness

Those bodies either to good or to evil.
If the form be blessing, the man is thankful;
If it be suffering, he is patient;
If it be cherishing, he is cheerful;
If it be bruising, he is full of lamentation!
Since all these forms are slaves of Him without form,
Why do they deny their Lord and Master?
They exist only through Him that is without form;
What, then, means their disavowal of their Sustainer?
This very denial of Him proceeds from Him,
This act is naught but a reflection from Himself!
The forms of the walls and roofs of houses
Know to be shadows of the architect's thought;
Although stones and planks and bricks
Find no entrance into the sanctuary of thought,
Verily the Absolute Agent is without form,
Form is only a tool in His hands.
Sometimes that Formless One of His mercy
Shows His face to His forms from behind the veil of Not-being,
That every form may derive aid therefrom,
From its perfect beauty and power.
Again, when that Formless One hides His face,
Those forms set forth their needs.
If one form sought perfection from another form,
That would be the height of error.
Why then, O simpleton, do you set forth your needs
To one who is as needy as yourself?
Since forms are slaves, apply them not to God,
Seek not to use a form as a similitude of God. 5
Seek Him with humbleness and self-abasement,
For thought yields naught but forms of thought.
Still, if you are unable to dispense with forms,
Those occurring independently of your thought are best. 6
The "Truth," which is our real self, lies hidden within our
phenomenal and visible self, and the Prophets reveal it to us.
"Now have we seen what the king saw at the first,

When that Incomparable One adjured us."
The prophets have many claims to our gratitude,
Because they forewarn us of our ultimate lot,
Saying, "What ye sow will yield only thorns;
If ye fly that way, ye will fly astray.
Take seed of us to yield you a good harvest,
Fly with our wings to hit the mark with your arrow.
Now ye know not the truth and nature of the 'Truth,' 7
But at the last ye will cry, 'That was the "Truth."'
The Truth is yourself, but not your mere bodily self,
Your real self is higher than 'you' and 'me.'
This visible 'you' which you fancy to be yourself
Is limited in place, the real 'you' is not limited.
Why, O pearl, linger you trembling in your shell?
Esteem not yourself mere sugar-cane, but real sugar.
This outward 'you' is foreign to your real ' you;'
Cling to your real self, quit this dual self.
Your last self attains to your first (real) self
Only through your attending earnestly to that union.
Your real self lies hid beneath your outward self,
For 'I am the servant of him who looks into himself.' " 8
"What a youth sees only when reflected in a glass,
Our wise old fathers saw long ago though hid in stones.
But we disobeyed the advice of our father,
And rebelled against his affectionate counsels.
We made light of the king's exhortations,
And slighted his matchless intimations.
Now we have all fallen into the ditch,
Wounded and crushed in this fatal struggle.
We relied on our own reason and discernment,
And for that cause have fallen into this calamity.
We fancied ourselves free from defects of sight,
Even as those affected by color-blindness.
Now at last our hidden disease has been revealed,
After we have been involved in these calamities."
"The shadow of a guide is better than directions to God,

To be satisfied is better than a hundred nice dishes.
A seeing eye is better than a hundred walking-sticks,
Eye discerns jewels from mere pebbles."
The princes ascertained the name of the lady depicted in the fort
from an old Shaikh, who warned them of the perils they would
encounter on their journey to China, and told them that the King of
China would not bestow his favor on those who tried to gain it by
tricks and clever stratagems, but solely on those who were
prepared to yield up their lives to him, according to the saying, "Die
before you die." This is illustrated by an anecdote of a Chief of
Bokhara, who made it a rule never to bestow his bounty on beggars
who asked for it, but only on those who awaited his pleasure in
silence. A certain Faqir tried many stratagems to evade this rule, but
his craft was at once seen through by the Chief, and turned to his
own confusion. The thesis that the unbought free grace of God is
superior to any blessing obtainable by human exertion and
contrivance is further illustrated by an absurd anecdote of two
youths, one of whom trusted for protection to his own contrivance,
and found it a broken reed. The Prophet said, "Two there are who
are never satisfied the lover of the world and the lover of
knowledge;" and he who loves knowledge will continue to trust in
his knowledge, in spite of all exhortations and experience. But the
eldest prince advised his brothers to risk the perils and persevere in
the journey, reminding them that "Patience is the key of joy."
Accordingly they abandoned their country and their parents, like
Ibrahim Adham, who renounced the throne of Balkh, and like the
old Arabian king Amru'l Qais, who fled from the pursuit of his
female adorers to seek the Spiritual Beloved in a far country.
How the princes discoursed with one another in figurative language
concerning their beloved mistress.
They told their secrets to one another in dark sayings,
Speaking beneath their breath in fear and trembling.
None but God was privy to their secrets,
None but Heaven was partner in their sighs.
Yea, they used technical expressions one to another,
And possessed intelligence to extract the sense.

The vulgar learn the words of this "language of birds," 9
And make boast of their mastery thereof;
But these words are only the outward form of the language,
The "raw" man is ignorant of the birds' meaning.
He is the true Solomon who knows the birds' language,
A demon, though he usurp his kingdom, is quite another.
The demon has taken upon him the form of Solomon,
His knowledge is fraud, not "what we have been taught."
When Solomon was blessed with inspiration from God,
He learned birds' language from "what we were taught."
But thou art only a bird of the air; understand then
That thou hast never seen the true spiritual birds!
The nest of the Simurgh is beyond Mount Qaf, 10
Not every thought can attain thereto;
Save thoughts which catch a glimpse thereof,
And after the vision are again shut off.
Yet not all shut off, rather intermitted for a wise end,
For the blessing abides, though shut off and hidden!
In order to preserve that body which is as a soul,
The Sun is veiled for a while behind a cloud;
In order not to melt that soul-like body,
The Sun withdraws itself as from ice.
For thy soul's sake seek counsel of these inspired ones. 11
Ah! rob not their words of their technical meanings!
Zulaikha applied to Yusuf the names of all things,
Beginning with wild rue and ending with frankincense.
She veiled his name under all other names,
And imparted her secret meaning to her confidants.
When she said, "The wax is melted by the fire,"
She meant, "My lover is wroth with me."
So when she said, "See, the moon is risen!"
Or, "Lo! the willow-bough is putting forth leaves;"
Or if she said, "The leaves quiver in the wind,"
Or, "The wild rue yields perfume as it burns;"
Or if she said, "The rose tells her tale to the Bulbul,"
Or, "The king sings his love-strain;"

Or if she said, "Ah! what a blessed lot!"
Or, "Who hath disturbed my heart's repose?"
Or if she said, "The water-carrier hath brought water,"
Or, "Lo! the sun emerges from the clouds;"
Or if she said, "Last night the victuals were boiled,"
Or, "The food was perfectly cooked;"
Or if she said, "My bread is without savor"
Or, "The heavens are revolving the wrong way;
Or if she said, "My head aches with pain,"
Or, "My headache is now relieved;"
If she gave thanks, 'twas for being united to Yusuf;
If she wailed, 'twas that she was separated from him.
Though she gave vent to thousands of names,
Her meaning and purport was only Yusuf;
Was she an hungred, when she pronounced his name,
She became filled and cheered by his nourishment.
Her thirst was quenched by Yusuf's name,
His name was spiritual water to her soul.
Was she in pain, by pronouncing his mighty name
At once her pain was turned into joy.
In the cold it was a warm garment;
Her lover's name accomplished all this through love.
Strangers may pronounce the "pure name" of God,
Yet it effects no such marvels, for they lack love.
All that 'Isa accomplished by the name of Jehovah,
Zulaikha attained through the name "Yusuf."
When the soul is intimately united with God,
To name the one is the same as naming the other.
Zulaikha was empty of self and filled with love of Yusuf,
And there flowed out of her jar what it contained.
The scent of the saffron of union made her smile,
The stench of the onion of separation made her weep.
Each to have in his heart a hundred meanings,
Such is not the creed of true love and devotion.
"The Friend" is to the lover as day to the sun,
The material sun is a veil over the face of the real day.

Whoso distinguishes not the veil from "The Friend's" face
Is a worshipper of the sun; of such a one beware!
"The Friend" is the real day, and daily food of lovers,
The heart and the heart's torment of His lovers.

After enduring many toils and misfortunes the three princes at last
arrived in the metropolis of China, and thereupon the eldest prince
expressed his intention of presenting himself before the king, as he
could wait no longer. His brothers tried to dissuade him from risking
his life, pointing out that if he acted on blind impulse and vain
conceit he would surely go astray, for "a conceit hath naught of
truth;" 12 and they further urged him to listen to the counsels of
the Pir, or Spiritual Director. But the eldest brother refused to be
dissuaded from his purpose, saying he would no longer hide his
passion for his beloved, like one who beats a drum under a blanket,
but would proclaim it openly, and take the risk of whatever might
ensue. He added that he was convinced that he should obtain his
desire in some way or other, if not in the way that he expected;
according to the text, "Whoso feareth God, to him will he grant a
prosperous issue, and will provide for him in a way he reckoned
not." 13 Seekers after God fancy that He is far from them, and that
they must travel far to reach Him; but these are both erroneous
suppositions; and just as arithmeticians work out true answers to
their problems by the "Method of Errors," 14 so must the seekers of
God from these errors work out the conviction that God is very nigh
to them that call upon Him faithfully. To illustrate this an anecdote
is told of a man of Baghdad who was in great distress, and who,
after calling on God for aid, dreamt that a great treasure lay hid in a
certain spot in Egypt. He accordingly journeyed to Egypt, and there
fell into the hands of the patrol, who arrested him, and beat him
severely on suspicion of being a thief. Calling to mind the proverb
that "falsehood is a mischief but truth a remedy," 15 he determined
to confess the true reason of his coming to Egypt, and accordingly
told them all the particulars of his dream. On hearing them they
believed him, and one of them said, "You must be a fool to journey
all this distance merely on the faith of a dream. I myself have many
times dreamt of a treasure lying hid in a certain spot in Baghdad,

but was never foolish enough to go there." Now the spot in Baghdad named by this person was none other than the house of the poor man of Baghdad, and he straightway returned home, and there found the treasure. And he gave thanks, and recognized how "God causes ease to follow troubles," 16 and how "Men hate what is good for them," 17 and how God delays the answer to prayer, and allows men to remain poor and hungry for a season, in order to make them call upon Him, even as the Prophet said, "My servant is a lute which sounds best when it is empty."

Why the answer to prayer is delayed.

Ah! many earnest suppliants wail forth prayers,
Till the smoke of their wailing rises to heaven;
Yea, the perfume of the incense of sinners' groans
Mounts up above the lofty roof of heaven.
Then the angels supplicate God, saying,
"O Thou that hearest prayer and relievest pain,
Thy faithful slave is bowing down before Thee.
He knows of none on whom to rely save Thee;
Thou bestowest favors on the helpless.
Every suppliant obtains his desire from Thee."
God makes answer, "The delay in granting his prayer
Is intended to benefit him, not to harm him.
His pressing need draws him from his negligence to me;
Yea, drags him by the hair into my courts.
If I at once remove his need he will go away,
And will be destroyed in his idle sports.
Though he is wailing with heartfelt cry of 'O Aider!'
Bid him wail on with broken heart and contrite breast.
His voice sounds sweet in my ears,
And his wailing and cries of' O God!'
In this way by supplication and lamentation
He prevails with me altogether."
It is on account of their sweet voices
That choice parrots and nightingales are jailed in cages.
Ugly owls and crows 18 are never jailed in cages;
Such a thing was never heard of in history.

The disappointments of the pious, be sure,
Are appointed for this wise purpose.

The eldest brother then delayed no longer, but rushed into the presence of the King and kissed his feet. The King, like a good shepherd, was well aware of the troubles and cravings of his sheep. He knew that the prince had abjured earthly rank and dignity through love for his daughter, even as a Sufi casts away his robe when overpowered by ecstatic rapture. The only reason why the prince had lagged behind in the race and not presented himself to the King before was that hitherto he had lacked the "inner eye" or spiritual sense which discerns spiritual verities, and had been consequently blind to the King's perfections. They who lack this inner spiritual sense can no more appreciate spiritual pleasures than a man lacking the sense of smell can enjoy the perfume of flowers, or a eunuch the society of fair women. But his eyes had now been opened by the King's grace, and he had escaped from the bondage of worldly lusts and illusions, and, taught by experience, had resolved never again to be led captive by them.

This is illustrated by the anecdote of the Qazi who was beguiled by the wife of a dwarf. The dwarf and his wife were very poor, and one day the dwarf said to his wife, "God has given you arched brows and arrowy glances and all manner of witchery; go and ensnare some rich man, so that we may extract money from him!" So the woman went to the court of the Qazi, pretending to have a grievance; and when she saw the Qazi she beguiled him, and induced him to pay her a visit at night. While the Qazi was sitting with her the dwarf returned home and knocked violently at the door, and the Qazi, in a great fright, hid himself in a large chest. The dwarf at once fetched a porter, and told him to take the chest to the bazar and sell it. On the way to the bazar the Qazi cried out to the porter to fetch the Deputy; and when the Deputy came he redeemed the chest for one hundred Dinars, and thus the Qazi escaped. Next year the woman went to the court and tried to seduce the Qazi a second time; but he said, "Begone; I have escaped from your toils once, and will not fall into them again. The action of the Deputy in freeing the Qazi reminds the poet of the saying of the Prophet, "Of him, of whom I am the master, 'Ali also is master," and is therefore able to free him from slavery.

The eldest prince at last fell sick of hope deferred, and gave up the ghost. But though he failed to obtain the King's daughter, the object of his earthly attachment, he obtained union with the King, the real spiritual object of his love, and the eternal fruition of dwelling in Him.

The joys of union with the Spiritual Beloved are inexpressible in speech.

In short, the King cherished him lovingly,
And he like a moon waned in that sun.
That waning of lovers makes them wax stronger,
Just as the moon waxes brighter after waning.
Ordinary sick persons crave a remedy for sickness
But the lovesick one cries, "Increase my waning!
I have never tasted wine sweeter than this poison,
No health can be sweeter than this sickness!
No devotion is better than this sin (of love),
Years are as a moment compared to this moment!"
Long time he dwelt with the King in this manner,
With burning heart, as a lively sacrifice.
Thus his life passed, yet he gained not the union He wished.
Patient waiting consumed him, his soul could not bear it;
He dragged on life with pain and gnashing of teeth.
At last life ended before he had attained his desire.
The form of his earthly Beloved was hidden from him;
He departed, and found union with his Spiritual Beloved.
Then he said, "Though she lacks clothes of silk and wool,
'Tis sweeter to embrace her without those veils.
I have become naked of the body and its illusions,
I am admitted into the most intimate union."
The story admits of being told up to this point,
Bat what follows is hidden and inexpressible in words.
If you should speak and try a hundred ways to express it,
'Tis useless; the mystery becomes no clearer.
You can ride on saddle and horse up to the sea-coast,

But then you must use a horse of wood (i.e., a boat).
A horse of wood is useless on dry land,
It is the special conveyance of voyagers by sea.
Silence is this horse of wood,
Silence is the guide and support of men at sea.
This Silence which causes you annoyance
Is uttering cries of love audible to the spiritual.
You say, "How strange the spiritual man is silent!"
He answers, "How strange you have no ears!
Though I utter cries, you hear them not;
Sensual ears, however sharp, are deaf to my cries."
The spiritual man, as it were, cries in his sleep,
Uttering thousands of words of comfort;
While the carnal man at his side hears nothing at all,
For he is asleep, and deaf to the other's voice.
But the perfect spiritualist who has broken his boat
Plunges into the sea as a fish of the sea (of Truth).
He is then neither silent nor speaking, but a mystery.
No words are available to express his condition.
That marvelous one is in neither of these states
'Twould be irreverent to explain his state more fully.
These illustrations are weak and inappropriate,
But no fitter ones are obtainable from sensible objects.
When the eldest prince died, the youngest was sick and could not
come; but the second brother came to the court to attend his
funeral. There the King observed him, and took pity on him and
entreated him kindly. He instilled into him spiritual knowledge of
the verities hidden beneath phenomenal objects, and conveyed to
him as deep a perception of spiritual truths as is not gained by a Sufi
after years of fasting and retirement from the world. It is a fact, that
when the pure spirit escapes from the bonds of the body, God gives
it sight to behold the things of the spirit. The logician denies the
possibility of this divine illumination of the heart, but he is confuted
by the Prophet, who swore "by the star" that the Koran was
revealed to him by divine illumination. 19 Those who cleave to their
heresy (Bid'at) and obstinate unbelief are like to incur the

punishment inflected on the tribe of 'Ad for disbelieving the Prophet Hud. 20 Earthly forms are only shadows of the Sun of the Truth, a cradle for babes, but too small to hold those who have grown to spiritual manhood. When the prince was thus nourished by the spiritual food given him by the King, which was such as the angels of heaven subsist upon, not the unspiritual food of Christians and those who give partners to God, he began to be puffed up with self-conceit, and forgot what he owed to the King, and rebelled against him. The King was cut to the heart by his ingratitude, which exactly resembled that of Nimrod. When Nimrod was an infant he was taken by his mother to sea, and the ship being wrecked, all that were in it perished, save only the infant Nimrod who was saved through the pity of Izrail, the Angel of Death. God spared him, and nurtured him without the aid of mother or nurse; but when he grew up he proved ungrateful, and was puffed up with self-conceit and egotism, and showed enmity against God and Abraham His servant. When the prince found himself cast off by the King he came to himself, and repented and humbled himself with deep contrition. The King then pardoned him; but his doom had already been decreed by God, and he was slain by the King he had injured, acknowledging the King's goodness to him with his latest breath. The death of the second prince.

In short, the vengeance of That Jealous One (God)
After one year bore him to the grave.
When the King awoke out of his trance to consciousness,
His Mars-like eyes shed tears of blood.
When that incomparable one looked into his quiver,
He saw that one of his arrow-shafts was missing.
He cried to God, "What has become of my arrow?"
God answered, "Thy arrow is fixed in his throat!"
That King, bountiful as the sea, had pardoned him;
Nevertheless his arrow had dealt him a mortal wound.
He was slain, and cried out with his last breath,
"The King is all in all, my slayer and my savior.
If he is not both these, he is not all in all;
Nay, he is both my slayer and my mourner!"

That expiring martyr also gave thanks,
That the King had smitten his body, not his spirit;
For the visible body must perforce perish,
Ere the spirit can live in happiness for evermore.
Though he incurred chastisement, it affected his body only,
And as a friend he now goes, free of pain, to his Friend.
Thus at first he clung to the King's stirrup,
But at last went his way guided by perfect sight.
Finally, the youngest brother, who was the weakest of all,
succeeded where his brothers had failed, and obtained his earthly
mistress, the king's daughter, as his bride, and the Spiritual Beloved
as well.
Here the Masnavi breaks off; but, according to the Bulaq edition,
the following conclusion was supplied by Jalalu-'d-Din's son, Bahau-
'd-Din Sultan Valad:
Part of the story remains untold; it was retained
In his mind and was not disclosed.
The story of the princes remains unfinished,
The pearl of the third brother remains unstrung.
Here speech, like a camel, breaks down on its road;
I will say no more, but guard my tongue from speech.
The rest is told without aid of tongue
To the heart of him whose spirit is alive.
*NOTES:
1. Koran lxvii. 10.
2. Surat, or "form," means picture, image, outward appearance as
opposed to reality, conception or "form of thought," the
"architypes" or "ideas" in the Divine mind, "the Substantial forms"
of the Realist philosophy. Here the poet runs through nearly all
these meanings.
3. Sale's Koran, p. 75, note.
4. i.e., the architypes in the "Intellectual Presence" or "world of
command," which are afterwards set forth in the "world of creation
or sensible objects.
5. See Koran xlii. 9.
6. i.e., the similitudes used in the Koran.

7. "The Truth," Al Haqq, the Divine Noumenon.

8. See Gulshan i Raz, Answer III., and the Hadis, "Whoso knows himself knows his Lord."

9. Koran xxvii. 16.

10. Simurgh, "Oiseau extraordinaire qui reside au Caucase," as M. Garcin de Tassy calls it, means "thirty birds" (Si murgh), and is used as a type of the Divine Unity which embraces all plurality.

11. i.e., the prophets and saints.

12. Koran x. 37.

13. Koran lxv. 2.

14. i.e., "The Rule of Position."Khulasat ul Hisab, Book iv.

15. Freytag, Arabum Proverbia, ii. 379.

16. Koran ii. 213.

17. Koran lxv. 7.

18. i.e., hardened sinners like Pharaoh.

19. Koran liii. 1.

20. Koran xlvi. 20.

Note on Apocryphal Supplements to the Masnavi.

In the Lucknow edition there follows an epilogue written by Muhammad Ilahi Bakhsh, giving a continuation of the story of the third brother, but nothing of the kind is found in any of the other editions.

The Bulaq edition adds a so-called Book VII., but this is known to be a comparatively recent forgery. Haji Khalfa says: "It is notorious that the Masnavi is contained in six books, but a seventh book has made its appearance, put forth by Ismail Dadah, the commentator. He also wrote a commentary on it, and therein replied with eloquence and strenuousness to those who denied its genuineness. He says in his commentary that when he came to write out his fifth volume in the year 1035 A.H., he met with Book VII. in a copy of the Masnavi dated 814 A.H. He bought it and read it through, and was satisfied that it was undoubtedly a composition of the author of the Masnavi. But the other Darveshes of the Maulavi order denied the genuineness of the Seventh Book." 1

The contents of this Seventh Book consist of comments on various texts and traditions, illustrated by stories of no interest. They have nothing in common with the Epilogue of Muhammad Ilahi Bakhsh, found in the Lucknow edition.

*NOTES:

1. Haji Khalfa, v. 377. Ismai1 was a Darvesh of the Maulavi order, surnamed Anguravi, from his native place Anguri, in Anatolia.

End of the book.

www.ingramcontent.com/pod-product-compliance
Lightning Source LLC
Chambersburg PA
CBHW060004300526
45794CB00003B/1085